SCHOLASTIC

NO BORING PRACTICE, PLEASE!

PARTS OF SPEECH

Reproducible Practice Pages PLUS Easy-to-Score Quizzes That Reinforce the Correct Use of Nouns, Verbs, Adjectives, Adverbs, and More

by Harold Jarnicki

New York • Toronto • London • Auckland • Sydney
New Delhi • Mexico City • Hong Kong • Buenos Aires

Teaching *Resources*

Cover by Jaime Lucero
Cover illustrations Mike Moran
Interior design by NEO Grafika
Illustrations by Kelly Kennedy

ISBN 0-439-53147-0
Copyright © 2005 by Harold Jarnicki
All rights reserved.
Printed in the U.S.A.

5 6 7 8 9 10   40   12 11 10 09 08 07

Table of Contents

Introduction

magine a classroom where students do not slump in their seats every time you announce it's time for grammar; where grammar lessons and practice bring exciting opportunities along with a couple of laughs and a little competition; where students get emotionally involved in grammar fundamentals, and improvement is proudly displayed by students and recognized by teachers and parents.

You might think such a classroom is merely a figment of my imagination or a fantasy of some ambitiously naive first-year education grad. I can boldly claim that such is not the case. I have been teaching for about 20 years and, with the help of some games, a few jokes, and other gimmicks, have witnessed students get excited about grammar, vocabulary, spelling, and more.

The No Boring Practice, Please! series is an extension of my classroom and one humble step toward helping kids do what comes naturally—learn. If you're ready to add spice to your grammar lessons, then this book is for you.

Carefully structured as a good basic course of study, the recipe for each lesson is simple. *No Boring Practice, Please! Parts of Speech* dishes up straight grammar practice with a dash (or splash) of fun. Inside you'll find a concoction of reproducible pages that cover nouns, proper nouns, verbs, adjectives, adverbs, prepositions, conjunctions, and more. Flavored with engaging illustrations and an edgy design, each practice page is easy for kids to swallow. Best of all, you can serve these pages with only a minimal amount of teacher instruction.

Each unit opens with a brief, simple explanation of a key concept in easy-to-understand language. Students are then challenged to apply what they are learning through practice pages. Next comes a review,

followed by a quick and easy-to-score quiz. Occasionally, you may want to add an extra exercise or practice test depending on students' progress, but the units are designed to stand on their own.

You may wonder what inspired me to write this book—and the rest of the No Boring Practice, Please! series. Let me start at the beginning. As a baby boomer's hyperactive kid, I wasn't a huge fan of school. Sitting at a desk most of the day was tough enough. Add a generous helping of dry grammar practice and my eyes would glaze over, roll back in my head, and send me into a near comatose state where hands on clocks ceased to move.

Years passed. After a less-than-stellar career in rock 'n' roll, I decided the teaching profession was a more lucrative gig. I had two specific goals: (1) to become the teacher I never had; and (2) to add a little rock 'n' roll to the school system.

Like it or not, we are teaching a new breed of children—one that watches more than four hours of values-distorting TV each day, plays mindless video games on a regular basis, and gobbles up entertainment far more than nutriment. We welcome these media-savvy kids into our classrooms and expect them to get excited about proper nouns, verb tense, degrees of comparison, and prepositional phrases. Let's get real!

This is what drives the No Boring Practice, Please! series. The series is academically sound and rich in language-skill development, but all this learning is disguised by a hip design and comical illustrations that have lots of kid appeal. Think of the series as whole-grain oats packaged in a box of tutti-frutti breakfast cereal.

I know that students can get excited about doing well in grammar, and I feel gratified to be part of the process. I hope the No Boring Practice, Please! series helps teach and inspire.

May the force be with you.

Sincerely,
Harold Jarnicki

Name _____

What Is a Noun?

Did you know that words belong to different groups? These groups are called **parts of speech**. **Nouns, verbs, adjectives,** and **adverbs** (to name a few) are all parts of speech.

Let's start with the noun.

Wondering if a word is a noun? Just place *a* or *the* in front of the word. If it makes sense, it's a noun!

A noun is a person, place, thing, or idea.

a cat (noun)   **the eat** (not a noun)
the experience (noun)

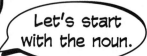

Most of the words in the Word Showcase are nouns. Write each one in the correct column of the Groovy Noun Chart.

Groovy Noun Chart

PERSON	PLACE	THING or IDEA	NOT A NOUN
Johnny	Sweden	computer	kindly

Word Showcase

	Atlantic Ocean	✔ kindly	speedy	farm
	playground	player	✔ computer	apple
	happiness	Africa	Rosa Parks	harder
✔ Johnny	is	freedom	boy	Wendy
school	teacher	swimming	elevator	town
candy	girl	Disneyland	green	oxygen
serious	bear	✔ Sweden	mayor	sneaky

Warning: Not all words are nouns.

Name _____

May I Introduce Proper Nouns?

A **proper noun** is the name of a particular person, place, or thing.

Pardon me, but did you know that a proper noun always begins with a capital letter, even when it doesn't begin a sentence?

People's names	Countries, states and provinces, cities and towns, schools, restaurants, stadiums, stores	Days and months, holidays, religions, titles, teams and clubs
Jack Frost	Oswego Free Academy	Saturday July
Tinker Bell	Peru California	San Francisco Giants

Proper Noun Awesome Treasure Hunt

A. People

❶ Name three people in your class. Write their first and last names:

_____

_____

_____

❷ Write your teacher's name:

_____

❸ Name three famous people:

_____

_____

B. Places

❶ Unscramble the names of these countries. Remember to capitalize them properly!

xeocmi	
adnaac	
sdettaietnsu	
yanek	

❷ Write your address:

_____

❸ Name two cities or towns you would like to visit:

_____ _____

❹ Write the name of your school:

_____

C. Things

❶ Fill in this chart with particular names of your favorite things. Then compare it with a friend's chart.

A Few of My Favorite Things	
My favorite song	
My favorite book	
My favorite TV show	
My favorite movie	
My favorite video game	
My favorite sports team	

❷ Unscramble these world religions. Remember to capitalize them properly!

smdaiju		mduhiins	
laism		udhidsbm	
itrinystchia			

Wacky Tales

Fill in each blank with the correct type of noun to complete this wacky fairy tale.

Remember: A **common noun** doesn't need to be capitalized.
A **proper noun** always needs to be capitalized.

Once upon a _____ in a land called _____ there lived a
            common noun   proper noun

_____. Her name was _____. Unfortunately, she was very sad
   common noun   proper noun

because she did not have a _____.
            common noun

One day a _____ came to visit her. His name was _____.
       common noun   proper noun

"I can help you get what you want," he said to her.

"That would be wonderful!" she exclaimed. "If you can do that, I will give you all the

_____ in _____."
   common noun   proper noun

So off he went, climbing _____ and fighting _____. He even
        common noun   common noun

visited the dangerous land of _____, where he was swallowed up by a slimy,
        proper noun

fire-breathing _____.
     common noun

Unfortunately, things just don't always work out.

The End

Name _____

What Is a Pronoun?

A **pronoun** is a word that replaces a noun.

 With a pronoun, you don't have to keep repeating the same noun over and over again.

A **personal pronoun** refers to a specific person or thing.

Personal pronouns: I, you, he, she, it, we, you, they

Read each sentence. Replace the repeated noun with a personal pronoun.

Example: Her name is Gina and ~~Gina~~ **she** is happy.

1. The door is squeaky when the door opens.

2. Sally is a good dancer because Sally practices a lot.

3. Dana, Khan, and Jack sang a song that Dana, Khan, and Jack all liked.

4. My family is going on a vacation because my family could use a break.

More Personal Pronouns

Just like nouns, some **personal pronouns** do an action and some receive the action.

I am talking to <u>her</u>.

The pronoun **I** is doing the action, while **her** is receiving the action.

She is talking to <u>me</u>.

Here, the pronoun **she** is doing the action, and **me** is receiving the action.

Personal pronouns that receive the action include: me, him, her, us, them.

Correct the pronouns in these sentences.

1. Jorge put he in the crib.

2. This book is for she.

3. The CD belongs to I.

4. Those bikes belong to they.

Name _____

Our Possessive Pronouns

These are all possessive pronouns:
mine, yours, his, hers, its, ours, theirs

Follow these examples to change the sentences below.

The slimy lizard *belongs to me*. ——————▶ The slimy lizard is *mine*.

The slimy lizard *belongs to you*. ——————▶ The slimy lizard is *yours*.

1. The slimy lizard *belongs to them*. ——▶ The slimy lizard is _____.

2. The slimy lizard *belongs to us*. ——▶ The slimy lizard is _____.

3. The slimy lizard *belongs to her*. ——▶ The slimy lizard is _____.

4. The slimy lizard *belongs to him*. ——▶ The slimy lizard is _____.

5. The slimy lizard *belongs to it*. ——▶ This is _____ slimy lizard.

Find 10 pronoun mistakes and correct them.

George ran across the street without looking. His almost got hit by a car.

The driver had to swerve to avoid he.

Him was so scared him face was as white as a ghost. Me heart was pounding, too.

"Me will never do that again," George said, "but that bike over there is me own."

"The bike just looks like it's you, George," me told him, "but it's me."

We're Pronouns Too!

You've met the usual pronouns: *he*, *she*, *we*, *it*, *him*, *her*, and more.
But did you know that *who*, *whom*, *whose*, *which*, and *what* are also pronouns? These are called **interrogative pronouns** and are used in questions.

Example: **Who** are you?
What is that?

This, *these*, *that*, and *those* are also pronouns. Called **demonstrative pronouns**, they point out persons or things.

Example: **These** are mine.
That belongs to my nana.

Then there are also *all*, *few*, *none*, *any*, *both*, *each*, *several*, *anyone*, *someone*, *somebody*, *everybody*, *nobody*, and other **indefinite pronouns** that do not refer to specific nouns.

Example: **Somebody** spilled the beans and I'll find out who.
Everybody has left for the day.

Circle all the pronouns in each sentence. Below each pronoun, write what type it is.

Example: I think these belong to nobody.

personal   demonstrative   indefinite

❶ That is not his, it's mine.

❷ Someone told her that we would be here.

❸ Which did he choose?

❹ There's nobody out there.

❺ Did anyone leave this behind?

I know what kind of pronoun that is!

Name _____

Verbs in Action

Verbs tell what something is doing. Verbs that show action are called **action verbs**.

Suzy <u>hit</u> the ball.
Mendel <u>ate</u> the sushi.
The kangaroo <u>jumps</u> high.

Choose a verb from the Action Verb Pool to complete each sentence. Every sentence should make sense.

1. My computer _____ again.

2. The deer _____ through the forest.

3. Her old truck _____ down the street.

4. Let's _____ to Queen Lilliputz.

5. Please _____ on tight!

6. Sometimes I _____ too much.

7. Goldfish _____ in the bowl.

8. Wilma _____ like a canary.

9. We _____ my bedroom purple.

10. Barney _____ good stories.

Action Verb Pool

wave	writes
hold	ran
painted	sings
chugged	talk
crashed	swim

Amazing Action Verbs

Make your verbs exciting! Use a thesaurus.

Complete each sentence with an amazing action verb.

❶ I _____ through the air.

❷ Nick _____ the building.

❸ Sophie _____ through the forest.

❹ We never _____ unless we ask first.

❺ They always _____ before dinner.

❻ I have been _____ for a long time.

Name _____

Linking Verbs

Linking verbs connect a noun, pronoun, or adjective to the subject that it describes or talks about.

subject   linking verb   complement

The pizza <u>was</u> cheesy.

Subject = person, place, or thing (who or what we are talking about)
Complement = words that come after a linking verb and tell more about the subject

The most common linking verb is the verb *to be,* which means "to exist." *Is, am, was, are, were, shall be,* and *will be* are all forms of *to be.*

Underline the linking verb and fill in the chart. Follow the example.

DRAW ARROWS TO CONNECT the subject and complement through the Linking Verb.	LINKING VERB Connects who or what we are talking about	SUBJECT What or whom we are talking about	COMPLEMENT What we are saying about our subject
1. The cheese <u>was</u> moldy.	was	cheese	moldy
2. I am president.			
3. She grew stronger.			
4. Detention seemed endless.			
5. The flowers smelled sweet.			
6. I feel nervous.			
7. The cake tasted yummy.			
8. Our team looks ready.			
9. The tree remained there.			
10. The alarm sounded loud.			

Helping Verbs

A **helping verb** is used before another verb to help make the meaning of the main verb clearer.

The Big List

Here's the big list of helping verbs. Try saying the entire list 10 times fast!

am, are, is, was, were, has, had, have, do, does, did, may, might, must, shall, will, can

Example: I <u>am</u> (climbing) a slippery flagpole.
Do you (climb) slippery flagpoles?
I <u>have</u> (climbed) slippery flagpoles.
I <u>have been</u> (climbing) slippery flagpoles all my life.

Help the Verbs!

Use the Helping Verbs and Main Verbs from the Verb Chart to complete the sentences. Use each verb only once.

❶ I _____ _____ on a lily pad.
helping verb   main verb

❷ She _____ _____ to Planet Neemoy.
helping verb   main verb

❸ We _____ _____ the giant artichoke.
helping verb   main verb

❹ Joe _____ _____ _____ since last Christmas.
helping verb   helping verb   main verb

❺ Nelly thinks she _____ _____ across the Pacific Ocean.
helping verb   main verb

❻ I _____ _____ ten bottles of Fruitzy Pop.
helping verb   main verb

❼ He _____ _____ over the brown lumps.
helping verb   main verb

❽ I _____ _____ to Arizona.
helping verb   main verb

VERB CHART

Helping Verbs	am	has	have	has	did	been	am	did	can
Main Verbs	flown	sitting	running	swim	singing	eat	drunk	jump	

Name _____

More Helping Verbs

These helping verbs are used in verb phrases to change the meaning of the main verb: **could**, **would**, **should**, **can**, **may**, **must**, **might**.

Check out how these helping verbs change the meaning of the main verb *jump*.

I'm jumping for joy!

You **jump** in the lake.

You **can jump** in the lake.

You **should jump** in the lake.

You **might jump** in the lake.

You **could jump** in the lake.

You **must jump** in the lake.

Choose a helping verb to complete each sentence.

I can do this!

1. _____ I go to the washroom?

2. I _____ climb up if I really tried.

3. You _____ get home before it gets dark.

4. She _____ come here if she leaves work early.

5. I know I _____ beat you in a race.

6. We _____ wait here for help.

7. You _____ not step on the thin ice or you will fall in.

8. How much wood _____ a woodchuck chuck?

9. He's so tired he _____ not get up for a while.

10. You _____ stay at my place if you want to.

Name _____

Get Tense With Verbs

A verb's **tense** shows when something has happened or will happen. Most verbs change form depending on the time of the action.

If the action is happening now, the verb is in the **present tense**.

I flap my wings.

If the action happened before (like yesterday), the verb is in the **past tense**.

I flapped my wings last week.

Writing a verb in the past tense can be as simple as adding **-ed**.

jump • • • • • • ▶ jumped

Sometimes you may have to double the last consonant before adding **-ed**.

flap • • • • • • ▶ flapped

Other times, you may have to change letters in the **middle** of the verb.

drive • • • • • • ▶ drove

If the action has not happened yet, the verb is in the **future tense**.

I will flap my wings next week.

Tense? Who says I'm tense?

One Last Thing: For singular nouns and pronouns (such as *he*, *she*, or *it*), add an **-s** to a present tense verb.

She **drives**.

Tense?

Complete the following verb tense chart.

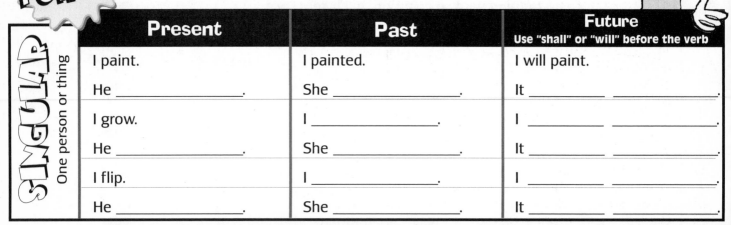

SINGULAR One person or thing	**Present**	**Past**	**Future** Use "shall" or "will" before the verb
	I paint.	I painted.	I will paint.
	He _____.	She _____.	It _____.
	I grow.	I _____.	I _____.
	He _____.	She _____.	It _____.
	I flip.	I _____.	I _____.
	He _____.	She _____.	It _____.

PLURAL More than one person or thing	**Present**	**Past**	**Future**
	We drive.	We _____.	We _____.
	We know.	We _____.	We _____.
	We laugh.	We _____.	We _____.

Déjà Vu X-Word Review

Use what you have learned about nouns and verbs to complete the crossword.

Across

4. *Is*, *am*, and *was* are forms of _____.
5. Verbs can express _____.
6. Major verb in a sentence
10. Kind of verb that helps the main verb make sense
12. A person's name always begins with a _____ letter.
14. "To be" verbs show that we _____.
15. Kind of pronoun that shows ownership
19. Kind of verb that connects what we are talking about
20. Word that replaces a noun
21. Belongs to them
22. More than one
23. "To be" verb that goes with *I*

Down

1. A pronoun replaces a noun instead of _____ it over and over.
2. In a sentence, this is what or whom we are talking about.
3. In a sentence, this is what we are saying about the subject.
6. Helping verb; rhymes with *night*
7. Person, place, or thing
8. Kind of noun that doesn't usually start with a capital letter
9. Belongs to me
11. Helping verb; ought to
13. *I*, *you*, *he*, and *she* are all examples of _____ pronouns.
15. Kind of noun that always starts with a capital letter
16. One
17. Words we put into grammar groups are parts of _____.
18. Action word

Let's Get Retro!
Nouns, Pronouns, and Verbs

Fill in the Blanks:

1. _____ are groups of words that have different functions.

2. A _____ is a person, place, thing, or idea.

3. _____ name specific persons, places, things, or ideas.

4. A _____ takes the place of a noun.

5. *I*, *you*, *he*, *she*, and *it* are examples of _____.

6. *Mine*, *yours*, *his*, *hers*, and *its* are examples of _____.

Quick Verb Review

Use the Puzzler Words to complete the puzzle.

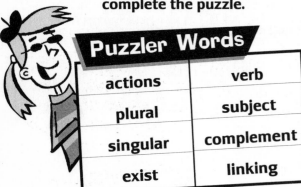

Puzzler Words

actions	verb
plural	subject
singular	complement
exist	linking

Across
2. Means "to be"
4. Many verbs show these.
6. Tells what something is doing
7. Only one
8. What we are saying about the subject

Down
1. Verb that connects
3. What or who we are talking about in a sentence
5. More than one

Check the Verb

Check the kind of verb the underlined word is.

	Action	"To be"	Linking	Helping	Not a verb
1. She <u>has</u> eaten a tree.					
2. This <u>is</u> good.					
3. <u>Squeeze</u> the bottle.					
4. We <u>should</u> go home now.					
5. Wait <u>for</u> me.					
6. Mandy <u>felt</u> happy.					
7. I <u>was</u> there until noon.					
8. I will <u>hold</u> that for you.					

QUICKIE QUIZ Nouns, Pronouns, and Verbs

Score: _____ /15

A Here Are the Questions: Write the answers on the blanks.

1. What kind of noun doesn't start with a capital letter? _____

2. What kind of noun always begins with a capital letter? _____

3. Which part of speech shows action? _____

4. Instead of repeating a noun over and over, what can you use? _____

5. What kind of verb helps main verbs make sense? _____

B Noun or Verb?

Circle the nouns. Underline the verbs.

Score: _____ /15

1. The cow ate the flowers.

2. The speedy runner can win the race.

3. A big fish still needs oxygen.

4. Sydney went to Australia.

5. Moisha sings and dances on stage.

I think you're getting this stuff!

C Proper Noun? Capitalize It!

Circle the proper nouns that should be capitalized.

Score: _____ /15

1. Let's all go to rayfield's diner for lunch.

2. jane lives in brazil.

3. i am jewish and she is moslem.

4. Today is tuesday, june 23.

5. graham goes to broadwater academy.

It's proper to capitalize the first letter of a sentence, too.

D Possessive Pronouns

Write the correct possessive pronoun in the blank.

Score: _____ /10

1. That belongs to them, so it is _____.

2. That belongs to him, so it is _____.

3. That belongs to us, so it is _____.

4. That belongs to me, so it is _____.

5. That belongs to you, so it is _____.

E Personal Pronouns

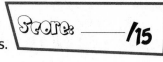

Score: _____ /15

Choose the best personal pronoun to replace the underlined nouns.
Write the pronoun above the underlined words.

1. Bo, you can go to the show with <u>Moe, Joe, and me</u>.

2. Here comes Auntie May. <u>Auntie May</u> is going to bake me a cake.

3. Pete eats trees. <u>Pete</u> eats trucks too.

4. Molly let me borrow the pencil, but <u>the pencil</u> belongs to Jill.

5. My brothers and sisters are getting on the bus. Later, <u>my brothers and sisters</u> will get off the bus.

F Missing "To Be" Verbs

Fill in each blank with the correct form of "to be."

1. I _____ on Cloud Nine yesterday.

2. They _____ at school tomorrow.

3. We _____ at the store yesterday.

4. She _____ at the movies now.

5. You _____ living in a zoo.

Score: _____ /10

G True or False

Write **T** for true and **F** for false.

_____ **1.** Verbs never show action.

_____ **2.** More than one person or thing is called singular.

_____ **3.** Proper nouns and pronouns are the same thing.

_____ **4.** Possessive pronouns show ownership.

_____ **5.** *Me* and *us* are personal pronouns.

Score: _____ /10

You did it!

H Do the Verb

Write the correct kind of verb in each blank. We included the first letter for each verb you need.

1. Marney b_____ angry when she heard the news.
linking verb

2. I h_____ watched hippos before.
helping verb

3. We s_____ all look both ways before crossing the street.
helping verb

4. It s_____ very noisy just because I had a headache.
linking verb

5. My mom said that I m_____ wait at home until she gets here.
helping verb

Score: _____ /10

Name _____

Much Ado About Adjectives awesome game

Adjectives are used to describe nouns. Adjectives can make your speech and writing interesting, fascinating, and totally illuminating!

beautiful day   **funky music**   **cool fashion**

An adjective gives a noun a more specific meaning. How?

Adjectives usually come before the nouns they describe, but not always.

1. An adjective tells **what kind**:

>   **big** book   **red** car
>
>   **cool** dude   **iced** coffee

2. An adjective tells **which one**:

>   **those** wheels   **this** kiwi
>
>   **that** disc   **these** earrings

3. An adjective tells **how many**:

>   **three** amigos   **some** shirts
>
>   **many** hours   **few** apples

Circle and ID

Circle the adjective in each sentence. Then check whether the adjective tells *what kind*, *which one*, or *how many*.

	What Kind	Which One	How Many
1. The yellow sunflowers sway in the wind.			
2. Many leaves have fallen from the tree.			
3. Those kids will surely win the contest.			
4. Mom loves green apples.			
5. That pencil belongs to Luis.			
6. I need to oil my squeaky bike.			
7. Norma owns three dogs.			
8. The TV is broken.			

Name _____

Outrageous Adjectives

Underline the nouns and circle the adjectives. Then replace each ordinary adjective with an incredible adjective. Beware: There may be more than one adjective in each sentence.

bashful   delightful
1. The (shy) boy sang a (nice) song.

The bashful boy sang a delightful song.

2. The mean dog was actually a gentle being.

_____

3. The shiny car glistened in the hot sun.

_____

4. I couldn't resist that sweet dessert.

_____

5. Dad won't go in that busy store.

_____

6. The odd lady was green yet beautiful.

_____

7. The bad storm caused bad damage.

_____

8. Brave pioneers lived through cold winters.

_____

9. Junior was a lucky child to avoid the awful accident.

_____

10. My old truck almost sank in the soft mud.

_____

Use a thesaurus!

Adverb Adventure

Adverbs modify verbs, adjectives, or even other adverbs.

Modify means to change something, usually only slightly.

Adverbs usually answer one of these questions.

How? How much? When? Where?

1. Jack jumped **merrily**.   *How* did Jack jump?
2. Jack jumped **frequently**.   *How much* did Jack jump?
3. Jack jumped **early**.   *When* did Jack jump?
4. Jack jumped **everywhere**.   *Where* did Jack jump?

Adverbs can make adjectives stronger.

How cold? Very cold!

adverb   **adjective**   **noun**

It was a very cold day.

The **noun** is *day*. The **adjective** tells us it was a *cold* day. The **adverb** tells us it was a *very* cold day.

The puppy ate very hungrily.

Two adverbs: **Very** tells us how **hungrily** the puppy ate.

Make the connection

Underline the verbs and circle the adverbs. Draw an arrow from the adverb to the verb it modifies. Identify what question the adverb answers: How? How much? Where? or When?

Hint: There may be more than one adverb. Adverbs are not always next to the verbs.

Example: Billy joyfully ran into the giant cream pie. **?** *HOW*

1. Katharine rode carefully through the busy streets. **?** _____

2. The clown cried wildly.   **?** _____

3. I slowly read the recipe for fruitcake.   **?** _____

4. The alarm rang loudly when the fire began.   **?** _____

5. The fish leaped high out of the water.   **?** _____

6. Gently, Dr. Eaton removed the bandage.   **?** _____

7. The jockey rode his horse there.   **?** _____

8. Earlier, Nikita ate the orange.   **?** _____

9. She finished her homework yesterday.   **?** _____

0. I spoke softly so the baby would sleep.   **?** _____

Look! Many adverbs end in -ly.

Oh, how lovely!

Fun With Adverbs

Word Search

Find 10 hidden adverbs.

Y	Q	D	T	Y	L	C	Y	W	E	L	L
L	K	V	S	L	Y	L	I	P	P	A	H
D	W	Q	A	R	W	L	O	U	D	L	Y
L	R	M	F	O	Y	L	L	A	Y	O	R
I	K	V	L	O	Y	L	T	F	I	W	S
W	M	S	U	P	E	R	B	L	Y	V	N

P___O___ ___ Y
S W ___ ___ ___ ___ ___ ___
W___L ___
S___P ___ ___ B ___ ___ ___
R___Y ___ ___ ___ Y
SL ___ ___ LY
H___ ___P ___ ___ ___ ___
L___U ___ ___ Y
W___ L D ___ ___ ___
F___ S ___

Use the adjectives and adverbs from the pool to complete the sentences. Make sure your sentences make sense!

1. This is an _____ _____ day.
   <small>adverb</small>   <small>adjective</small>

2. Alec is wearing a _____ _____ costume.
   <small>adverb</small>   <small>adjective</small>

3. Austin is _____ _____.
   <small>adverb</small>   <small>adjective</small>

4. In this _____ _____ bus, we'll be late.
   <small>adverb</small>   <small>adjective</small>

5. Tuesday was _____ _____ for spring.
   <small>adverb</small>   <small>adjective</small>

6. Jack jumped over the _____ _____ candlestick.
   <small>adverb</small>   <small>adjective</small>

7. The sea was _____ _____.
   <small>adverb</small>   <small>adjective</small>

8. That _____ _____ dog is frightening.
   <small>adverb</small>   <small>adjective</small>

9. The princess held _____ _____ roses.
   <small>adverb</small>   <small>adjective</small>

10. The _____ _____ witch cackled with nastiness.
    <small>adverb</small>   <small>adjective</small>

Adverb Pool	Adjective Pool
unbelievably	decorate
ferociously	red
totally	slow
slowly	wicked
truly	beautiful
brightly	clever
amazingly	vicious
incredibly	stormy
horribly	warm
unusually	burning

24 No Boring Practice, Please! **Parts of Speech**

Dare to Compare

Adjectives and adverbs are also used to compare things. The most common way to compare things is to add **-er** or **-est** to the adjective or adverb. Check out this chart:

Positive Degree
Describing **ONE** thing

Mars is **big**.

Comparative Degree
Comparing **TWO** things

Saturn is **bigger** than Mars.

Superlative Degree
Comparing **THREE** or **MORE** things

Jupiter is the **biggest** planet.

Adjectives with two or more syllables sometimes use **more** or **most** to compare things. So do adverbs that end in *-ly*.

Comparative Degree: She is **more cheerful** than Susan.
Superlative Degree: She is the **most cheerful** person in our class.

 Be the Smartest!

Complete the Degrees of Comparison Chart using *-er*, *-est*, *more*, or *most*. Check out the examples before you begin.

POSITIVE	COMPARATIVE	SUPERLATIVE
• small	smaller	smallest
• intelligent	more intelligent	most intelligent
1. beautiful		
2. bright		
3. young		
4. handsome		
5. worried		
6. quietly		
7. rapidly		
8. far		
9. late		
10. early		

Degrees of comparison chart

 Rule Breakers!

Some adjectives follow their own rules. Here are some of these big-time rule breakers:

good, better, best   **bad, worse, worst**
little, less, least   **many, more, most**

Déjà Vu X-WORD Review

You are incredibly smart!

Use your brain power to complete this adjective and adverb puzzle.

Let's review adjectives and adverbs!

Across

1. You have more, so I have _____.
4. When using an adjective to describe one thing, use the _____ degree.
8. Most adverbs end in these two letters.
9. I was good, but she was _____.
11. An adverb is not always right _____ the verb.
12. They describe nouns.
13. A question that adverbs answer
15. Another question that adverbs answer
17. That was bad, but this was the _____ of all.

Down

2. When using an adjective to compare three or more things, use the _____ degree.
3. When using an adjective to compare two things use the _____ degree.
5. "It is a very hot day." In this sentence, the adverb is modifying an _____.
6. Adverbs can modify other _____.
7. Modify can mean _____.
10. In grammar, another word for *describe*
14. What an adjective describes
16. The most common question answered by an adverb is _____.

Name _____

Let's Get Retro!
Adjectives and Adverbs

Degrees of Comparison: Fill in the chart with the correct adjectives.

Positive	Comparative	Superlative
	better	
		worst
pretty		
		tiniest
far		
		earliest
	less	
	more	

• •What Modifies What?

**Underline the nouns and double underline the verbs. Circle the adjectives
and box the adverbs. Draw an arrow from the adjective to the noun it
modifies. Draw an arrow from the adverb to the verb it modifies.**

Example: The (funny) clown leaped [merrily] into a (giant) marshmallow.

1. I carefully painted the white picket fence.

2. Harpo almost scored the winning goal.

3. The big, old wooden sign fell down.

4. Carefully chew the slippery snails.

5. Roaring thunderously, the powerful bulldozer effortlessly moved humongous boulders.

*Review your work
and get ready for
the Quickie Quiz!*

An Unexpected Mission

Complete the story using adjectives and adverbs where needed. Have fun, but make sure the story makes sense!

It all began one _____ day. I had _____ woken up
adjective   adverb

from a _____ sleep when in through my bedroom window came a
adjective

_____ creature.
adjective

"My name is Shmee!" it announced _____. "I come to your
adverb

_____ planet to _____ eat ice cream. I _____
adjective   adverb   adverb

want you to take me to the _____ ice-cream parlor you know of."
adjective

After recovering from _____ shock, I got dressed and
adjective

_____ tiptoed out the backdoor with Shmee.
adverb

We went to the _____ ice-cream parlor in our _____ town.
adjective   adjective

I told Shmee to _____ wait in the _____ bushes so that no one
adverb   adjective

would see him.

We had a _____ time. He _____ tried many
adjective   adverb

_____ flavors. There was _____, _____ fudge.
adjective   adjective   adjective

He loved it so much he did a _____ flip. Then when he
adjective

sampled _____, _____ bubble gum, he
adjective   adjective

laughed _____ like a hundred _____
adverb   adjective

monkeys. I guess his very favorite flavor had to be

_____, _____, _____ ice
adjective   adjective   adjective

cream because after he tasted that, he shook _____
adverb

until he disappeared. I never did see Shmee again.

Name: _____

Adjectives and Adverbs

A ## True or False: Write **T** for true and **F** for false.

_____ 1. Adverbs describe nouns.

_____ 2. In a sentence, you can have two adjectives in a row.

_____ 3. An adverb can modify another adverb.

_____ 4. An adjective can modify another adjective.

_____ 5. Modify means "to change slightly."

_____ 6. *Where* is the most common question answered by an adverb.

_____ 7. The superlative degree of comparison usually ends in *-er*.

_____ 8. Adjectives describe nouns.

_____ 9. Most adjectives end in *-ly*.

_____ 10. In a sentence, you can have two adverbs in a row.

B # Identify the Part of Speech

Identify whether the underlined word is an adjective or adverb.

1. Larry ate a <u>big</u> supper.	**adjective**	**adverb**
2. I will wait <u>patiently</u> for you.	**adjective**	**adverb**
3. She is a <u>fast</u> runner.	**adjective**	**adverb**
4. Baxter can run <u>fast</u>.	**adjective**	**adverb**
5. I <u>hardly</u> bumped you.	**adjective**	**adverb**
6. He wants to eat that <u>juicy</u> peach.	**adjective**	**adverb**
7. Chew that bubble gum <u>carefully</u>.	**adjective**	**adverb**
8. <u>Slippery</u> snails are easy to swallow.	**adjective**	**adverb**

C # What's the Question?

Write the question (*how, how often, when, where*) each adverb is answering.

1. skips hurriedly _____

2. eats anywhere _____

3. flies early _____

4. walks silently _____

5. eats always _____

D Degrees of Comparison

Complete the chart with the correct degree of each adjective.

Score: _____ /20

POSITIVE	COMPARATIVE	SUPERLATIVE
good		
bad		
beautiful		
many		
far		

E More Degrees of Comparison

Score: _____ /1

Fill in the blanks with the correct adjective and degree of comparison. Follow the example.

Example: Mike was great, but Ali was the ___*greatest*___ of all.

1. I have only a little, but you have even _____ than I do.

2. This is a bright light, but that one is _____.

3. Prince Humperdink was handsome, but Prince Charming was _____.

4. Bob has many cards, but I think you have _____.

5. This kitten is still very young, but that one is even _____.

Score:

_____ /16

F What Modifies What?

Underline the nouns and double underline the verbs. Circle the adjectives and box the adverbs. Draw an arrow from the adjective to the noun it modifies. Draw an arrow from the adverb to the verb it modifies.

Example: The (sad) child cried silently.

1. Grandpa easily painted the old car.

2. The red and white sign stands out.

3. In the clear blue sky, cottony clouds rambled.

4. The powerful bulldozer growled loudly.

Name _____

Major Wacky Tale!

Complete the story below. Fill in the blanks with correct part of speech. Make sure the story makes sense!

This was one crazy adventure!

A True Story My Uncle Told Me

My _____ Uncle _____ tells some _____ stories. But one
       adjective   *proper noun*   *adjective*

of the _____ ones he has ever told me was about the time he went for a walk one
       superlative adjective

_____ morning down in the swamps of _____.
  adjective   *proper noun*

He always took his _____ _____ _____ with him. He never
                      adjective   *noun—pet*   *proper noun—pet's name*

went anywhere without _____ _____.
                         adjective   *proper noun—pet's name*

Well, as the story goes, the two of them had just _____ over the _____,
                                                       verb   *noun*

across the _____ and down to the _____. This was the place they loved the
             noun   *noun*

best, yet as soon as the two got down there, _____ _____ started acting
                                                 adjective   *proper noun—pet's name*

_____ _____.
    adverb   *adverb*

First, he began _____ _____. A couple of seconds later, he was
                   verb ending in "ing"   *adverb*

_____ like a _____ _____ that had just eaten too many
verb ending in "ing"   *adjective*   *noun*

_____.
 plural noun

Then something incredible happened. _____ began _____ and
                                       proper noun—pet's name   *verb ending in "ing"*

_____. Soon he was _____ around as if on a _____
verb ending in "ing"   *verb ending in "ing"*   *adjective*

_____. He didn't stop until his _____ fell off. Then his _____
   noun   *noun*   *noun*

turned yellow and a _____ was _____ from his ears.
                       noun   *verb ending in "ing"*

Uncle _____ was _____. He just turned around and _____.
         proper noun   *adjective*   *verb*

He didn't stop until he got home. When he got there, _____ was _____
                                                        proper noun—pet's name   *verb ending in "ing"*

on his favorite _____ as if nothing had happened.
                   noun

Well, that's a true story. At least, that's the way Uncle _____ tells it.
                                                              proper noun

Name _____

Prepositions make connections.

Presenting Prepositions

A **preposition** shows the relation of a noun or pronoun to other words in a sentence. It's like a **linking word** that connects nouns (or pronouns) with other words.

A preposition can indicate **position** ●●●●●●●●●●●●●► Gronk stood **between** Blatt and Zitt.

A preposition can indicate **direction** ●●●●●●●●●●●● ► Birdman climbed **up** the wall.

A preposition can indicate **time** ●●●●●●●●●●●●●●► I will make a sandwich **after** you.

A preposition can indicate **cause** (reason for) ●●●●●●► Eat your mush **because** it is good for you.

A preposition can indicate **possession** (ownership) ●●●► This is a collection **of** mine.

Preposition Pool

Check out this chart of common prepositions.

POSITION	DIRECTION	TIME	CAUSE	POSSESSION
across	above	about	**but** (meaning "except")	for
against	around	after	except	of
along	below	at	since	
behind	down	before		
beside	from	during		
between	in	past		
beyond	over	until		
by	through			
into	to			
off	toward			
on	under			
with	up			

Some prepositions can indicate more than one thing. For example, on can indicate position and time. For can indicate possession and time.

Plunk the Prepositions

2 easy steps!

❶ Choose a preposition from the **Preposition Pool** column indicated.

❷ In the blank, place a preposition that makes sense.

Example: Indicating **time**   Beano played ____after____ school.

1. Preposition indicating **possession**   Marcel will wait _____ you.

2. Preposition indicating **position**   Please put that _____ the wall.

3. Preposition indicating **possession**   That is one _____ Mom's best dishes.

4. Preposition indicating **direction**   Get _____ from there now!

5. Preposition indicating **cause**   You can eat it, _____ I can't.

6. Preposition indicating **position**   I would love to travel _____ our solar system to another galaxy.

7. Preposition indicating **position**   Let's all dive _____ the swimming pool.

8. Preposition indicating **time**   You can go _____ I do.

9. Preposition indicating **direction**   Gretel ran _____ the gingerbread house and out the door.

10. (1) Preposition indicating **time**;   _____ the game, I fell _____ my seat.
    (2) Preposition indicating **position**   (1)   (2)

Position the Prepositions

T	U	O	B	A	N	M	O	L	P
N	T	Y	R	W	O	R	V	F	A
U	O	F	O	R	V	T	E	F	S
L	P	D	F	J	N	M	R	O	T

BONUS

On the back of this paper, write a sentence for each preposition you find.

Find 11 prepositions in the word grid. The first letter of each preposition is provided at right.

b_____   f_____   p_____

a_____   d_____   o_____

f_____   o_____   o_____

o_____   u_____

Name _____

Prepositional Phrases

A phrase is a group of words. A **prepositional phrase** is a phrase that begins with a preposition and ends with a noun or pronoun.

Two kinds of prepositional phrases:
1. adjective phrase
2. adverb phrase

The Adjective Phrase

An adjective modifies a noun, so an **adjective phrase** does the same thing!

Ajax was **in shape**.

In shape is what **Ajax** (proper noun) is, and **in** is the preposition that begins the phrase.

 Use a prepositional phrase from the Adjective Phrase Pool to complete each sentence. Circle the preposition that begins the phrase.

Adjective Phrase Pool
to the king
on her head
for you
for lunch
with brown fur

1. That money _____ is in here.

2. Carla will eat a frog _____ .

3. The dog _____ can fly.

4. Jody can stand _____ for 10 seconds.

5. Those colorful chickens belong _____ .

The Adverb Phrase

You know that an adverb can modify a verb. An **adverb phrase** can do the same thing!

Bob ran **into the bag**.

Into the bag tells where Bob **ran** (verb), and **into** is the preposition that begins the phrase.

Get This! An adverb answers the question *how*, *where*, or *when* about a verb. *How* can also mean *how much* or *how many*. On this page, the adverb phrases modify only verbs.

 Use a prepositional phrase from the Adverb Phrase Pool to complete each sentence. Circle the preposition that begins the phrase and circle the question the phrase answers.

		Adverb Phrase Pool
1. Zip is _____ .	how? where? when?	**through the hole**
2. Norton wrote _____ .	how? where? when?	**until the cows come home**
3. Let's dance _____ .	how? where? when?	**to the flagpole**
4. Climb _____ .	how? where? when?	**in the morning**
5. My tongue is frozen _____ .	how? where? when?	**between Chip and Skip**

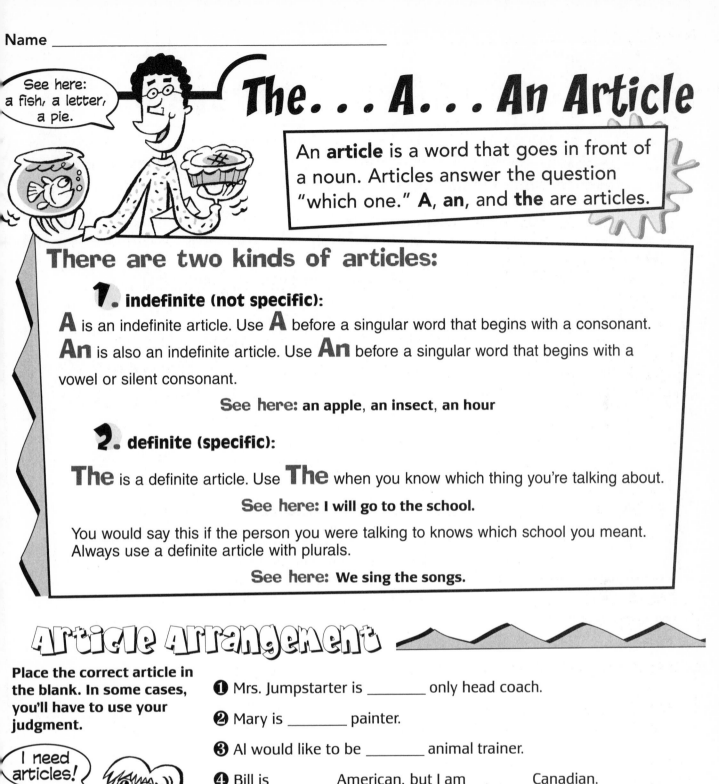

See here: a fish, a letter, a pie.

The... A... An Article

An **article** is a word that goes in front of a noun. Articles answer the question "which one." **A**, **an**, and **the** are articles.

There are two kinds of articles:

1. indefinite (not specific):

A is an indefinite article. Use **A** before a singular word that begins with a consonant.
An is also an indefinite article. Use **An** before a singular word that begins with a vowel or silent consonant.

See here: an apple, an insect, an hour

2. definite (specific):

The is a definite article. Use **The** when you know which thing you're talking about.

See here: I will go to the school.

You would say this if the person you were talking to knows which school you meant. Always use a definite article with plurals.

See here: We sing the songs.

Article Arrangement

Place the correct article in the blank. In some cases, you'll have to use your judgment.

I need articles!

❶ Mrs. Jumpstarter is _____ only head coach.

❷ Mary is _____ painter.

❸ Al would like to be _____ animal trainer.

❹ Bill is _____ American, but I am _____ Canadian.

❺ This is _____ only way to Grandma's house.

❻ Dad listens to _____ radio.

❼ Please turn off _____ lights.

❽ The apples are $2.00 _____ pound.

❾ _____ police are checking speeders.

❿ _____ school has _____ playground.

The Conjunction's Function

A **conjunction** is a word that joins words or groups of words.

These **coordinating conjunctions** connect words to words or phrases to phrases.

AND: used to add information together. It is the most common conjunction.
Example: My bike is gold **and** blue. I like to eat cookies **and** milk

BUT: used to note a difference
Example: Wendy lost the game, **but** she is still happy.

YET: often used to replace *but*, but not always
Example: Wendy lost the game, **yet** she played well.

OR: used to suggest a choice. It is sometimes used with **either**.
Example: Do you want chocolate **or** vanilla?
Either come in **or** stay outside.

NOR: used in place of *or* when it is used with **neither**
(*Neither* actually means "not either.")
Example: The weather was neither hot **nor** sunny.

SO: used to give a reason for doing what has just been mentioned
Example: Hold on tightly **so** you don't fall.

FOR: used primarily as a preposition, but can be used in place of *because*
For is not commonly used as a conjunction.
Example: Juliet is sad, **for** she wants Romeo.

It's okay to begin a sentence with *AND* or *BUT*. Just make sure it really is the strongest way to express your idea!

Conjunction Junction Crossword

Test your knowledge of coordinating conjunctions with this crossword.

Across
3. The most common conjunction
5. Paired with *neither*
6. Can replace *but*
7. A conjunction _____ words or groups of words.
9. Used to suggest a choice
11. Can be partnered with *or*

Down
1. It's okay to begin this with *and* or *but*
2. Can replace the word *because*
4. Not either
8. Can be used to give a reason for something
10. Usually used to note a difference

Name _____

Conjunctions Continued

Complete each sentence with a word from the Conjunction Pool.
Use each conjunction only once.

Conjunction Pool

but
nor
and
or
so
but
or
and
for
so

❶ Should I stay _____ should I go?

❷ Neither Ricky _____ Ulysses will get a chance.

❸ To get to the beach, we will take a car, a train, _____ a plane.

❹ Dodo is shy, _____ he still likes to perform on stage.

❺ My computer is broken _____ don't bother sending me email.

❻ Please put olives _____ anchovies on my pizza.

❼ Mom will help, _____ she really needs to rest first.

❽ Either we start our project today _____ tomorrow.

❾ Please clean up _____ we can go out and play.

❿ Watch out Caesar, _____ the Cyclops is hungry!

Wacky Tale Quickie

Complete the sentences using the correct parts of speech.

Have you seen the movie called "_____ _____
                                               article   adverb

_____ _____ "?
   adjective   noun

You must read "_____ _____ _____
                   preposition   article   adverb

_____ _____ ."
   adjective   noun

My favorite country-and-western song is " _____ Can _____
                      noun   verb

_____ _____ Can't _____
   conjunction   pronoun   verb

_____ _____ _____ Tonight."
  preposition   article   noun

Wow! Interjections

Interjections are short expressions found at the beginning of a sentence. They express excitement or emotion.

Awesome! I love my new bike.
Oh, we're having pizza again.

Interjections that show extreme excitement or emotion are followed by an exclamation point.

Cool! We're going to Costa Rica.
Ouch! That hurts.

A comma follows interjections that don't show extreme feelings or excitement.

Ah, that feels good.
Hey, where are you going?

Hey! Dive in!

Interjections Pool

Radical!	Whoa!	Oh boy!	Cool!	Oops!
Well!	Far out!	Sweet!	Help!	Uh-oh!
Awesome!	Oh!	Yahoo!	Totally!	Yuck!
Excellent!	Stop!	Boom!	Yippee!	Eek!
No way!	Wow!	Yikes!	Darn!	Hooray!
Rats!	Bravo!	Super!	Hey!	Ouch!
	Groovy!	Yes!		

Complete each sentence using an interjection from the box.

_____ I must have slipped.   _____ You did a great job.

_____ I'm not going.   _____ It's too dangerous.

_____ We won!

Complete these sentences. Decide if you need a comma or an exclamation point.

Awesome _____.

Yahoo _____.

Eek _____.

Oh boy _____.

Excellent _____.

Hint: If you can't answer a question, look back at earlier pages.

Across

1. The most common conjunction
3. More than one
6. A group of words
9. A part of speech that joins a group of words
10. A conjunction that helps explain a difference
11. A short emotional expression usually found at the beginning of a sentence
12. Kind of article used before a singular word that begins with a vowel or consonant
14. A conjunction used to suggest that you have a choice
15. An interjection can end with this punctuation

Down

1. Kind of prepositional phrase that modifies a noun
2. Kind of article always used with plurals
3. These link nouns with other words in a sentence
4. Kind of prepositional phrase that modifies a verb
5. Prepositions *for* and *of* indicate this
7. *The*, *a*, or *an*
8. This preposition can indicate position
13. Conjunction used instead of *because*
16. Article used before a word that begins with a vowel

Let's take a trip down Memory Lane!

Name _____

Let's Get Retro!
Prepositions, Articles, and More

Inject an Interjection
Complete the sentences with your own interjections.

_____! We won.

_____, before it's too late.

_____! I love that song.

_____, we missed the bus.

_____! I won the lottery.

_____, I'm not going.

_____, that's amazing.

_____, I'm sorry I did that.

_____! It's a monster!

_____! That is so cool!

Take Your Pick! Circle the correct part of speech for each underlined word.

❶ <u>Wow</u>, that icicle is so cool!   **a.** conjunction   **b.** preposition   **c.** article   **d.** interjection

❷ A moose jumped in <u>the</u> window.   **a.** conjunction   **b.** preposition   **c.** article   **d.** interjection

❸ I got a present <u>from</u> Uncle Shlitzie.   **a.** conjunction   **b.** preposition   **c.** article   **d.** interjection

❹ Stand <u>between</u> the squirrels.   **a.** conjunction   **b.** preposition   **c.** article   **d.** interjection

❺ Bill <u>and</u> Dave will perform tricks.   **a.** conjunction   **b.** preposition   **c.** article   **d.** interjection

❻ I was really hungry <u>so</u> I ate the TV.   **a.** conjunction   **b.** preposition   **c.** article   **d.** interjection

❼ <u>The</u> little girl chased the gorilla.   **a.** conjunction   **b.** preposition   **c.** article   **d.** interjection

❽ <u>Yuck</u>, here comes a hairball!   **a.** conjunction   **b.** preposition   **c.** article   **d.** interjection

Placing Prepositions: Choose the correct preposition from the Prep Box to complete each sentence.

Example: Do you want to jump *into* that pit of vile glop? (*Indicating position*)

1. I have one million dollars _____ you. (*Indicating possession*)

2. There is a monkey _____ your head. (*Indicating direction*)

3. I could eat two dump trucks _____ I am very hungry. (*Indicating cause*)

4. Junior, stay in your room _____ you finish your push-ups. (*Indicating time*)

5. Can you fit _____ the hole in that donut? (*Indicating direction*)

6. I will wait _____ the purple ice-cream truck. (*Indicating position*)

7. Who knocked Humpty _____ the wall? (*Indicating position*)

Prep Box
since
by
above
until
off
through
for

Conjunction Functions

1. Two conjunctions that function as prepositions are _____ and _____.

2. A conjunction is a word that _____ words or groups of words together.

Scrambled!

Unscramble the conjunctions then use them to complete the sentences below.

tub:_____ **ro:**_____ **os:** _____

tye: _____ **fro:**_____ **dan:**_____ **ron:**_____

1. Do you want snails _____ beetles in your soup?

2. It is summer, _____ it is snowing!

3. Neither Wilma _____ Betty can find a dinosaur.

4. I will shake the tree _____ you can catch the coconut.

5. Rocky can't remember his name _____ he bonked his head.

6. Horatio chased the truck, _____ he couldn't catch it.

7. "Give me a kiss _____ a big hug," said Auntie Fanny.

The Art of Articles Fill in the blanks with the correct answers.

A. **1.** The only definite article is _____. Definite means _____.

2. Two indefinite articles: _____ and _____.

B. Choose the best article for each blank.

1. Mary had _____ big, fat lamb.

2. I want to go to _____ hockey game.

3. _____ president of _____ United States will make his speech now.

4. The Cool Cats are _____ only team to beat us.

5. I want to be _____ doctor or _____ actor when I grow up.

Name: _____

Prepositions, Articles, and More

Read and think carefully!

A True or False: Write **T** for true and **F** for false.

_____ 1. *It* is a preposition.

_____ 2. With a plural, always use a definite article.

_____ 3. *Or* is the most common conjunction.

_____ 4. A comma or an exclamation point can follow an interjection.

_____ 5. A preposition begins a prepositional phrase.

_____ 6. An interjection is usually one word.

_____ 7. Conjunctions join words together.

_____ 8. We use *a* before words that begin with vowels.

_____ 9. *Definite* is the opposite of *specific*.

_____ 10. *A*, *an*, and *the* are articles.

Score: _____ /20

B ID the Part of Speech: Circle the correct part of speech for each underlined word.

1. Take a pickle <u>from</u> the jar.

   a. conjunction   **b. interjection**   **c. preposition**   **d. article**

Score: _____ /10

2. Here comes <u>the</u> pig.

   a. conjunction   **b. interjection**   **c. preposition**   **d. article**

3. <u>Awesome</u>! I love it!

   a. conjunction   **b. interjection**   **c. preposition**   **d. article**

4. You should step <u>over</u> the heap.

   a. conjunction   **b. interjection**   **c. preposition**   **d. article**

5. Squeeze the sponge <u>so</u> the water comes out.

   a. conjunction   **b. interjection**   **c. preposition**   **d. article**

C Define It: Prepositions can indicate five things. What are they?

1. _____   4. _____

2. _____   5. _____

3. _____

Score: _____ /10

D The Art of Articles   Score: _____ /20

a. Complete the sentences.

1. The only definite article is _____.

2. *A* and *an* are called _____ articles.

b. Choose the best article for each sentence.

3. Where did you hide _____ money?

4. A flower is plant, but a chicken is _____ animal.

5. That movie theater is down _____ street.

6. I would love to see _____ live dinosaur.

7. _____ Queen of England doesn't always wear her crown.

8. He is _____ only one who finished.

9. We left _____ hour ago.

10. Write _____ story about Tinkerbell.

E Conjunction Function   Score: _____ /40

a. Fill in each blank correctly.

1. Two conjunctions that also function as prepositions are _____ and _____.

2. A conjunction is a word that _____ words or groups of words.

b. Write the seven conjunctions.

❶ b _____   ❷ o _____   ❸ s _____   ❹ y _____   ❺ f _____   ❻ a _____   ❼ n _____

c. Use each of the above conjunctions once to complete each sentence.

1. You can play if you can throw _____ catch.

2. Caesar come here, _____ I need you.

3. I didn't finish, _____ I got most of it done.

4. Neither Snap _____ Crackle can see Pop.

5. It's hot, _____ I'm going swimming.

6. I am tired, _____ I can't sleep.

7. Which would you like, apples _____ pears?

I never would have believed something like this could happen if it hadn't happened

to me. I _____ _____ home _____ _____
       helping verb   main verb   preposition, position   noun, place

when all of a sudden a _____, _____, _____
             adjective   adjective   adjective

_____ came _____ toward me! Of course, I _____
    noun   verb   verb, past tense

_____ _____ as _____ as I could. I mean this
   conjunction   verb, past tense   adverb

_____ was the _____, _____ _____ I've
 noun, same as above   adjective, superlative   adjective, superlative   noun

ever seen!

    As I _____ _____, I saw a _____. I
             helping verb   main verb   noun

_____ _____ it. There, I waited _____ I thought it was
  verb, past tense   preposition, direction   preposition, time

_____. I _____ _____ in the _____.
   adjective   verb, past tense   adverb   noun

Minutes passed. _____, I _____ _____
                  adverb   verb, past tense   conjunction

_____ out. Was _____ _____ gone? I
  verb, past tense   article   noun

_____ _____ and _____. I didn't _____
   adverb   verb, past tense   verb, past tense   verb

_____ _____.
 indefinite pronoun   noun

"_____!" I _____ to myself. "I'm _____ I'm
  interjection   verb, past tense   adjective

_____."
  adjective

    Just then, _____ _____ _____ _____
               article   noun   verb, past tense   preposition, position

me. I _____! I couldn't stand it anymore! I _____ to the
     verb, past tense   verb, past tense

_____. "_____!" I _____. "_____ do you
  noun   interjection   verb, past tense   interrogative pronoun

_____ _____ me?"
  verb   preposition, position

_____ _____ _____ _____
  article   noun   verb, past tense   conjunction

_____ me. "Nothing," said _____ _____.
 verb, past tense   article   noun

"_____ just wanted to _____ you."
 personal pronoun   verb

I _____ _____. To this day, I still
  verb, past tense   adverb

can't believe this happened to me.

What Is a Noun? (p. 6)

Person	Place	Thing or Idea	Not a Noun
Johnny	Sweden	computer	kindly
teacher	school	candy	serious
girl	Atlantic Ocean	happiness	is
player	playground	bear	swimming
Rosa Parks	Africa	freedom	speedy
boy	Disneyland	elevator	green
mayor	farm	apple	harder
Wendy	town	oxygen	sneaky

May I Introduce Proper Nouns? (pp. 7–8)

A. People
1, 2, 3. Answers will vary.

B. Places
1. Mexico; Canada; United States; Kenya
2, 3, 4. Answers will vary.

C. Things
1. Answers will vary.
2. Judaism; Islam; Christianity; Hinduism; Buddhism

Wacky Tales: Common and proper nouns will vary.

What Is a Pronoun? (p. 9)

Fix It!
1. it
2. she
3. they
4. we

Try It!
1. him
2. her
3. me
4. them

Our Possessive Pronouns (p. 10)

Fix It!
1. theirs
2. ours
3. hers
4. his
5. its

Fix It Up!
George ran across the street without looking. He almost got hit by a car. The driver had to swerve to avoid him.

He was so scared his face was as white as a ghost. My heart was pounding, too.

"I will never do that again," George said, "but that bike over there is mine."

"The bike just looks like it's yours, George," I told him, "but it's mine."

We're Pronouns Too! (p. 11)

1. That – demonstrative; his – possessive; it's – personal; mine – possessive
2. Someone – indefinite; her – personal; we – personal
3. Which – interrogative; he – personal
4. nobody – indefinite
5. anyone – indefinite; this – demonstrative

Verbs in Action (p. 12)

Get Into Action!
1. crashed
2. ran
3. chugged
4. wave
5. hold
6. talk
7. swim
8. sings
9. painted
10. writes

Amazing Action Verbs: Answers will vary.

Linking Verbs (p. 13)

Draw Arrows	Linking Verb	Subject	Complement
1. The cheese <u>was</u> moldy.	was	cheese	moldy
2. I <u>am</u> president.	am	I	president
3. She <u>grew</u> stronger.	grew	She	stronger
4. Detention <u>seemed</u> endless.	seemed	Detention	endless
5. The flowers <u>smelled</u> sweet.	smelled	flowers	sweet
6. I <u>feel</u> nervous.	feel	I	nervous
7. The cake <u>tasted</u> yummy.	tasted	cake	yummy
8. Our team <u>looks</u> ready.	looks	team	ready
9. The tree <u>remained</u> there.	remained	tree	there
10. The alarm <u>sounded</u> loud.	sounded	alarm	loud

Helping Verbs! (p. 14)

Answers may vary. Possible answers:
1. am sitting
2. has flown
3. did eat
4. has been singing
5. can swim
6. have drunk
7. did jump
8. am running

More Helping Verbs! (p. 15)

Answers will vary. Possible answers:
1. May
2. can
3. should
4. might
5. can
6. should
7. should
8. would or could
9. may
10. could

Get Tense About Verbs (p. 16)

Present	Past	Future
I paint.	I painted.	I will paint.
He paints.	She painted.	It will paint.
I grow.	I grew.	I will grow.
He grows.	She grew.	It will grow.
I flip.	I flipped.	I will flip.
He flips.	She flipped.	It will flip.
We drive.	We drove.	We will drive.
We know.	We knew.	We will know.
We laugh.	We laughed.	We will laugh.

Déjà Vu X-Word Review (p. 17)

Let's Get Retro! Nouns, Pronouns, and Verbs (p. 18)
Fill in the Blanks
1. Parts of speech
2. noun
3. Proper nouns
4. pronoun
5. personal pronouns
6. possessive pronouns

Quick Verb Review

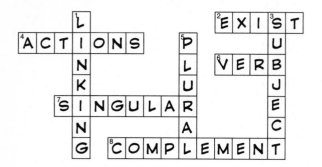

Check the Verb
1. helping
2. to be; linking
3. action
4. helping
5. not a verb
6. linking
7. to be; linking
8. action

Quickie Quiz: Nouns, Pronouns, and Verbs (pp. 19–20)
A. Here Are the Questions
1. common noun
2. proper noun
3. verb
4. pronoun
5. helping verb

B. Noun or Verb?
1. cow, flowers – noun; ate – verb
2. runner, race – noun; can win – verb
3. fish, oxygen – noun; needs – verb
4. Sydney, Australia – noun; went – verb
5. Moisha, stage – noun; sings, dances – verb

C. Proper Noun? Capitalize It!
1. Rayfield's Diner
2. Jane, Brazil
3. I, Jewish, Moslem
4. Tuesday, June
5. Graham, Broadwater Academy

D. Possessive Pronouns
1. theirs
2. his
3. ours
4. mine
5. yours

E. Personal Pronouns
1. us
2. She
3. He
4. it
5. they

F. Missing "To Be" Verbs
1. was
2. will be
3. were
4. is
5. are

G. True or False
1. F
2. F
3. F
4. T
5. T

H. Do the Verb
1. became
2. have
3. should
4. sounded
5. may

Much Ado About Adjectives (p. 21)
1. yellow – what kind
2. Many – how many
3. Those – which one
4. green – what kind
5. That – which one
6. squeaky – what kind
7. three – how many
8. broken – what kind

Outrageous Adjectives (p. 22)
Adjectives will vary.
2. The mean dog was actually a gentle being.
3. The shiny car glistened in the hot sun.
4. I couldn't resist that sweet dessert.
5. Dad won't go in that busy store.
6. The odd lady was green yet beautiful.
7. The bad storm caused bad damage.
8. Brave pioneers lived through cold winters.
9. Junior was a lucky child to avoid the awful accident.
10. My old truck almost sank in the soft mud.

Adverb Adventure (p. 23)
1. Katharine rode carefully through the busy streets. ? How
2. The clown cried wildly. ? How

Fun With Adverbs (p. 24)
Word Search

poorly
swiftly
well
superbly
royally
slowly
happily
loudly
wildly
fast

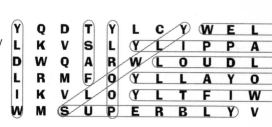

Fill It In!
Answers may vary. Possible answers:
1. amazingly beautiful
2. brightly decorated
3. truly clever
4. incredibly slow
5. unusually warm
6. slowly burning
7. unbelievably stormy
8. ferociously vicious
9. totally red
10. horribly wicked

Dare to Compare (p. 25)

Positive	Comparative	Superlative
beautiful	more beautiful	most beautiful
bright	brighter	brightest
young	younger	youngest
handsome	more handsome	most handsome
worried	more worried	most worried
quietly	more quietly	most quietly
rapidly	more rapidly	most rapidly
far	farther	farthest
late	later	latest
early	earlier	earliest

Déjà Vu! X-Word Review (p. 26)

(crossword puzzle with answers: LESS, POSITIVE, COMPARATIVE, CHANGE, SUPERLATIVELY, ADJECTIVE, ADVERB, BETTER, BESIDE, MODIFY, ADJECTIVES, WHEN, NOUN, WHERE, WORST)

Let's Get Retro! Adjectives and Adverbs (pp. 27–28)
Degrees of Comparison

Positive	Comparative	Superlative
good	better	best
bad	worse	worst
pretty	prettier	prettiest
tiny	tinier	tiniest
far	farther	farthest
early	earlier	earliest
little	less	least
many	more	most

What Modifies What?

1. I carefully painted the white picket fence.
2. Harpo almost scored the winning goal.
3. The big, old wooden sign fell down.
4. Carefully chew the slippery snails.
5. Roaring thunderously, the powerful bulldozer effortlessly moved humongous boulders.

An Unexpected Mission: Answers will vary.

Quickie Quiz: Adjectives and Adverbs (pp. 29–30)
A. True or False?

1. F	3. T	5. T	7. F	9. F
2. T	4. F	6. F	8. T	10. T

B. Identify the Part of Speech
1. adjective
2. adverb
3. adjective
4. adverb
5. adverb
6. adjective
7. adverb
8. adjective

C. What's the Question?
1. how
2. where
3. when
4. how
5. how often

D. Degrees of Comparison

Positive	Comparative	Superlative
good	better	best
bad	worse	worst
beautiful	more beautiful	most beautiful
many	more	most
far	farther	farthest

E. More Degrees of Comparison
1. less
2. brighter
3. more handsome
4. more
5. younger

F. What Modifies What?
1. Grandpa easily painted the old car.
2. The red and white sign stands out.
3. In the clear blue sky, cottony clouds rambled.
4. The powerful bulldozer growled loudly.

Major Wacky Tale! (p. 31)
Answers will vary.

Presenting Prepositions (p. 32)
Plunk the Prepositions
1. for
2. against, behind, beside, on, by
3. of
4. up, out
5. but
6. beyond, across, from
7. into
8. when, after, before
9. through
10. During, After; off, from

Position the Prepositions

by
about
from
of
for
down
over
up
past
off
on

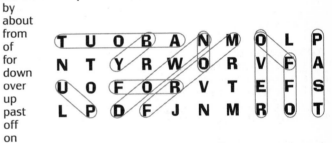

Prepositional Phrases (P. 34)
Do This
Answers may vary. Possible answers:
1. for you
2. for lunch
3. with brown fur
4. on her head
5. to the king

Try This!
Answers may vary. Possible answers:
1. between Chip and Skip (where)
2. in the morning (when)
3. until the cows come home (when)
4. through the hole (where)
5. to the frozen flagpole (where)

The … A … An Article (p. 35)

1. the	3. an	5. the	7. the	9. The
2. a	4. an, a	6. the	8. a	10. The, a

The Conjunction's Function (p. 36)

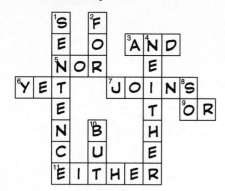

Crossword solution:
- S E
- F O A N D
- N O R E
- Y E T J O I N S
- E N O R
- N B H E
- C U E
- E I T H E R

Conjunctions Continued (p. 37)

1. or	4. but	7. but	10. for
2. nor	5. so	8. or	
3. and	6. and	9. so	

Wacky Tale Quickie
Answers will vary.

Wow! Interjections (p. 38): Answers and sentences will vary.

Déjà Vu! X-Word Review (p. 39)

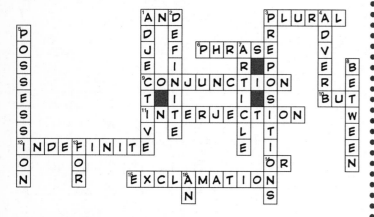

Let's Get Retro! Prepositions, Articles, and More (pp. 40–41)
Inject an Interjection: Answers will vary.

Take Your Pick!

1. d	4. b	7. c
2. c	5. a	8. d
3. b	6. a	

Placing Prepositions

1. for	4. until	7. off
2. above	5. through	
3. since	6. by	

Conjunction Functions
1. but, for
2. joins

Scrambled!
but, or, so, yet, for, and, nor

1. or	4. so	7. and
2. yet	5. for	
3. nor	6. but	

The Art of Articles
A. 1. the; specific
2. a; an
B. 1. a
2. a or the
3. The, the
4. the
5. a, an

Quickie Quiz: Prepositions, Articles, and More (pp. 42–43)
A. True or False?

1. F	4. T	7. T	10. T
2. T	5. T	8. F	
3. F	6. T	9. F	

B. ID the Part of Speech

1. c	4. c
2. d	5. a
3. b	

C. Define It
1. position
2. direction
3. time
4. cause
5. possession

D. The Art of Articles

1. the	4. an	7. The	10. a
2. indefinite	5. the	8. the	
3. the	6. a	9. an	

E. Conjunction Function
a. 1. but, for
2. joins
b. 1. but
2. or
3. so
4. yet
5. for
6. and
7. nor
c. 1. and
2. for
3. but
4. nor
5. so
6. yet
7. or

One More Wacky Tale! (p. 44)
Answers will vary.